jB B79t
Tallman, Edward.
Garth Brooks

DO NOT REMOVE
CARDS FROM POCKET

ALLEN COUNTY PUBLIC LIBRARY
FORT WAYNE, INDIANA 46802

You may return this book to any agency, branch,
or bookmobile of the Allen County Public Library.

DEMCO

Straight
from the
Heart

Garth Brooks

Straight from the Heart

Garth Brooks

By Edward Tallman

DILLON PRESS
New York

Maxwell Macmillan Canada
Toronto

Maxwell Macmillan International
New York Oxford Singapore Sydney

Photo Credits

Front cover: Gary Gershoff/Retna Ltd.
Back cover: AP-Wide World Photos
Interior photographs courtesy of Steve Lowry, with much thanks from the editor.

Book design by Carol Matsuyama

Library of Congress Cataloging-in-Publication Data

Tallman, Edward
Garth Brooks : straight from the heart / by Edward Tallman. — 1st ed.
p. cm. — (A Taking part book)
Discography: p.
Includes index.
Summary: A biography of the successful country singer.
ISBN 0-87518-595-9
1. Brooks, Garth—Juvenile literature. 2. Country musicians—United States—Biography—Juvenile literature. [1. Brooks, Garth. 2. Musicians. 3. Country music.] I. Title. II. Series.
ML3930.B855T3   1993
782.42'1642'092—dc20
[B]

Allen County Public Library
900 Webster Street
PO Box 2270
Fort Wayne, IN 46801-2270

93-10214

Copyright © 1993 by Dillon Press

All rights reserved. No part of this book may be reproduced or transmitted in any form or by any means, electronic or mechanical, including photocopying, recording, or by any information storage and retrieval system, without permission in writing from the Publisher.

Dillon Press
Macmillan Publishing Company
866 Third Avenue
New York, NY 10022

Maxwell Macmillan Canada, Inc.
1200 Eglinton Avenue East
Suite 200
Don Mills, Ontario M3C 3N1

Macmillan Publishing Company is part of the Maxwell Communication Group of Companies.

First edition

Printed in the United States of America

10 9 8 7 6 5 4 3 2 1

Contents

Introduction: What Is a Garth Brooks?..................7
One   Growing Up in Yukon..................11
Two   Burnin' Both Ends of the Night..................21
Three Nashville..................27
Four The Phenomenon Begins..................35
Five *Ropin' the Wind*..................45
Conclusion: Welcome to the Nineties..................55
Discography..................62
Index..................63

Introduction

What Is a Garth Brooks?

In the late summer of 1991 the Nashville office of Capitol Records was in a state of frenzy. Two million copies of the new Garth Brooks album were scheduled to arrive in record stores nationwide on September 23. Thousands of posters had to be mailed, and packages of three Garth video clips were being readied for release as well. The marketing blitz for what was soon to be known as the Garth Brooks Phenomenon was underway!

This was unprecedented. Recordings by Madonna and Paula Abdul always shipped in millions of copies. But they were pop singers supported by large corporations. Capitol, on the other hand, was a relatively small company. And Garth Brooks? He was a *country* singer. A chunky, balding guy who dressed like a ranch hand.

Through hard work and good fortune, Garth's album *Ropin' the Wind*, his third in three years, was on the shelves of record stores at the beginning of the last full week of September. By September 28 more than 2.5 million copies

The king of country music smiles at the world.

Garth Brooks Straight from the Heart

had been sold: sold not just in the traditional markets for country, the South and Southwest, but in big cities, too. Garth Brooks was selling albums in Boston, New York, Chicago, and Los Angeles. And his album was rushing out of stores in the suburbs of every large community of the United States and on college campuses, too.

This kind of success was amazing for a performer most people had never even heard of. Even other musicians were surprised. The heavy metal band Metallica had held the number one position on *Billboard*'s album chart for several weeks with their album *Metallica*. When Garth Brooks knocked the group out of the top spot, Lars Uhlrich, Metallica's drummer, asked, "What is a Garth Brooks?"

The answer? Garth Brooks was the *first* country singer to make an album that *debuted* at number one on the pop album charts. The *first* country singer to make an album that would sell more than eight million copies. The *first* country singer to achieve mass popularity on the scale of performers like Michael Jackson, Madonna, and Guns N' Roses. The *first* country singer to be worshiped by his fans the way Frank Sinatra had been idolized in the 1940s and Elvis

Garth's fans go wild as he waves from the stage.

Presley was swooned over in the 1950s.

Garth is simply the most successful singer in the history of country music. But sales figures and popularity do not answer the question: Who is Garth Brooks?

One

Growing Up in Yukon

"We had music around the house twenty-four hours a day."

—Garth Brooks

Troyal Garth was born on February 2, 1962, the youngest of six children in the Brooks household. Both Garth's mother, Colleen (Carroll) Brooks, and his father, Troyal Raymond Brooks, had been married before. One child was Ray's from his first marriage, and Colleen brought her three kids to the family when she married Ray. Colleen and Ray then had two boys together, Garth and Kelly.

Fifteen years separate the oldest child from Garth. He has four brothers—Kelly and Mike Brooks and Jim and Jerry Smittle—and a sister, Betsy Smittle. Growing up in a family with strict but loving parents, the Brooks kids never thought of themselves as "half brothers" or "half sisters." "We don't believe in the term," Garth says. "There were a lot of fights in town because of that term."

Garth's mom, Colleen Brooks

Garth Brooks Straight from the Heart

Garth inherited his love of performing from his mother. "If I have any talent," he says, "It comes from her." Colleen was a country singer in the 1950s. She appeared on a popular radio and television show and had recorded for Capitol Records. But when Ray asked her to become a full-time mother, Colleen agreed to give up her career.

Still, she made music—country music—an important part of the household. It wasn't hard to do, for Ray Brooks loved country music, too. He and Colleen had fallen in love while listening to songs by artists like Hank Williams and George Jones. At picnics and holiday get-togethers, Colleen played guitar and led the entire family in ringing sing-alongs. "We had music around the house twenty-four hours a day, it seemed," recalls Garth.

Although the Brooks family was happy and close-knit, life wasn't easy for Garth growing up in Yukon, a suburb on the outskirts of Oklahoma City. His father's paychecks from the Unocal oil company, where he worked as an engineer, afforded no luxuries for a young family the size of Ray's and Colleen's. Also, the cities and towns that flowered on the American frontier could be rough-and-tumble places, where the people loved

Garth with Colleen and Troyal Brooks

music that tells about the sorrows caused by drinking, fighting, and broken homes.

"Unfortunately, violence for me has always been a way of life," admits Garth. "It's something very real where I come from. I think Oklahoma City led the world in homicides per year—really—when I was growing up; they would average one or two a day. You'd turn on the news, and someone had been killed. It was no big thing. Violence was a way of life the same way love and

Garth Brooks Straight from the Heart

happiness was. Death, after all, is as much a part of living as being born." Some of the violence Garth encountered growing up would later find its way into his song lyrics.

Garth's father also had a temper with a very short fuse. "If I could wrap my dad up in two words," Garth says, "it would be thundering tenderness. He's a man with the shortest temper I ever saw, and at the same time, he's got the biggest heart." Garth explains that he learned from his father that "you gotta be thankful for what you got and treat people like you want to be treated." But in the Brooks household, Garth has said, it was his "dad who called all the shots and had all the last words."

By the time he enrolled at Yukon High School, Garth Brooks was an outgoing young man who liked people and wanted very much for people to like him. You would think the hottest man in the music business would have spent his time practicing the guitar or writing songs. But not Garth. He loved sports and failed to become a good banjo player because he spent his time playing football and baseball and training to become a track star. His sister, Betsy, who now plays in Garth's band, is the family's best instrumentalist.

Garth was one of Yukon High's most popular students. He

Garth's sister, Betsy, who is also his bass player, signs autographs for fans after a show.

was quarterback of the football team, a pitcher for the baseball team, a track-and-field star, and a member of the school's "in crowd." But even though he was one of the cool kids, Garth didn't make anyone feel left out. Because he was friendly to everyone

Garth participates in a story hour with a group of young fans.

and liked to make people laugh, Garth was well-liked by all of his classmates, including those who were shy or simply did not stand out from the crowd. Garth's teachers remember him as a polite, down-to-earth young man with a confident air and a mature understanding of himself. He did not study as hard as some of the other students, but he loved to read and write and take an active, vocal part in his English classes.

Although he is a country superstar, Garth Brooks listened to more than just country music when he was a teenager. His favorite musicians were James Taylor and Dan Fogelberg, who wrote and performed insightful folk songs that had modern rhythms and bright, popular melodies. Garth was also a fan of rock groups like Boston, Kiss, Journey, Queen, Fleetwood Mac, and REO Speedwagon.

In the 1970s many rock bands dressed in exotic costumes, and groups like Kiss painted their faces with layers of makeup. In concerts at large arenas, these bands entertained their fans with loud music and spectacular stage shows. Multi-colored strobe lights fanned over the stage, which often was blanketed in clouds of smoke that billowed from behind the band. The performers cavorted wildly, dancing and delighting

Garth Brooks Straight from the Heart

the audiences—all in an effort to reward their fans with a spectacle that would not soon be forgotten.

Garth loved this showmanship and never forgot it. Later he would treat *his* fans to laser light shows and onstage antics, like swinging from a rope as he sang and smashing his guitar into one of his bandmate's guitars. "Through junior high, I had every Kiss album there was," Garth recalls. "The late seventies rock shows probably influenced my live show the most, the visual stuff."

One day Garth was driving around in his car when a beautiful song came on the radio. That song was "Unwound," by a young singer named George Strait from his album *Strait Country*. It reminded Garth how powerful the "passion and emotion" of the best country music could be. "That's the exact moment it all changed," Garth says. "I became a George wannabe and imitator for the next seven years."

As his high-school days drew to a close, Garth, like most teenagers, had no idea what he wanted to do with his life. Sports, music, dating girls, and having a good time with friends were his main interests. While he enjoyed sports, Garth knew that he lacked the talent to become a professional athlete. And his mother knew all about the disappointment and the hardship faced by would-be musicians who try to break into show business. "Mom tried to discourage our interest in music as a career," recalls Garth. "Her advice was, 'Don't get in it.'"

For a time Garth considered joining the United States Marine Corps, as his father had as a young man. Ray, however, talked Garth out of a military career. He wanted his youngest child to attend college and study for a career in a high-paying industry. So, after graduating from Yukon High School in the spring of 1981, Garth enrolled at Oklahoma State University.

Two

Burnin' Both Ends of the Night

Garth Brooks admits that he "ran from responsibility as a kid." While majoring in advertising and marketing at Oklahoma State University, which is in Stillwater, about 50 miles from Oklahoma City, Garth was no more studious than he had been in high school. He practiced his guitar playing and sang once in a while at Shotgun's Pizza Parlor, a popular student hangout near the campus. But most of the students who knew Garth in Stillwater remember him as an athlete.

Standing six feet tall and weighing 185 pounds, Garth lifted weights as a hobby and could bench press more than 300 pounds. He made the Oklahoma State Cowboys' track-and-field team as a javelin hurler, which he could throw some 200 feet. Garth earned a partial athletic scholarship and competed for the Cowboys in the Big Eight Conference against teams from other large schools like the University of Nebraska, Oklahoma University, and the University of Colorado.

Once again, Garth proved to be a popular guy on campus. His peers liked him for his easygoing, down-to-earth ways, his

Garth enjoys a game of softball with his crew between shows.

Garth Brooks Straight from the Heart

sense of humor, and his genuine interest in other people. He wore casual clothes—sweat pants, T-shirts, baseball caps, and tennis shoes—but when he went out at night, he dressed up in pressed denims, boots, and a cowboy hat.

Because Garth was likable and mature, he was hired as a bouncer at a local nightclub called Tumbleweeds. A bouncer's job is to maintain order and keep people from starting fights. Garth's parents worried about their son's safety, but Garth's diplomatic manner and low-key personality always kept him out of trouble.

One night at Tumbleweeds a fight broke out in the ladies' room. When he went to investigate, Garth found a tall blond woman—with her fist stuck in the wall. "I missed," she explained to the surprised Garth.

Her name was Sandy Mahr. She had taken a swing at a woman who accused Sandy of flirting with her ex-boyfriend. Garth Brooks had been a ladies' man since high school. But now he found himself smitten by a pretty Oklahoma State coed, a former rodeo rider who had just broken a wall with her fist. Garth and Sandy soon started dating. He liked her spunk and fighting spirit. Before long, Garth Brooks was a one-woman man.

In his senior year at Oklahoma State, Garth failed to qualify

Garth and Sandy

for the conference track-and-field finals. He was disappointed. He had competed for OSU in each of the two previous years. One of his coaches tried to put matters in a positive light. He told Garth, "Now you can get on with what you really want to do."

The problem was Garth still didn't know what it was he wanted to do. He would graduate in the spring of 1985 with a degree in advertising. He knew he was serious about Sandy. He also knew that, even as a little boy, he had liked the spotlight,

Garth warms up before a concert.

liked being the center of attention. And now it was singing that made people notice him. Other than that, Garth's future was as uncertain as it had been four years before when he had left Yukon for Stillwater.

In the summer of 1984 Garth had performed in Oklahoma City at an audition held by Opryland USA, a theme park located in Nashville, Tennessee. Promoters for Opryland USA had been impressed with Garth and offered him a job singing country standards—popular songs that are known by all country music fans—in Nashville, the capital of country music. But Garth's parents had frowned on the idea. They persuaded him to return to school and finish his degree. Colleen and Ray Brooks told their son he would more likely find heartbreak than success in trying to become a successful country music entertainer.

Now, in the summer of 1985, Garth thought once again of Nashville. With his college degree in hand and no idea of what the future held, he left Sandy behind in Stillwater and set out for the city of his dreams.

Three

Nashville

"If you're gonna play in the big league, you've gotta be where they're swingin' the bats."
—Garth Brooks

Standing in the rain on the balcony of his motel room, Garth felt too foolish to cry, too "stupid," he later recalled, to pity himself. Instead, he let the rain wash away the childish dreams that brought him to Nashville. "It was like every raindrop was laughing at me," Garth said.

Just a day or two before, Garth was half expecting to see his name written up on every water tower in town as he arrived, brimming with confidence. A friend of Garth's got him an interview with Merlin Littlefield, an executive at ASCAP, the powerful agency that collects fees for songwriters. Garth played him a demo—short for *demonstration*—tape he had recorded of his songs, confident that he would quickly find a job.

But Mr. Littlefield was not encouraging. He explained that thousands of talented singers and songwriters descend on

Garth takes the stage for another night of fun and music.

Garth Brooks Straight from the Heart

Nashville every year, each one believing that she or he needs only a little luck to become famous. Very few if any of those hopefuls will ever step inside a recording studio, said Mr. Littlefield.

The harsh truth of Merlin Littlefield's words hit home when a well-known songwriter interrupted Garth's meeting. He needed $500 to repay a debt. Garth was shocked. This successful man had to beg for $500? "I make that much in a week just playing nights in Oklahoma," Garth blurted. The man just looked at him and said, "Then go home."

"There's nothing like an idiot with confidence," Garth said, looking back on his first trip to Nashville. "I came here thinking that country music needed me, that there was a hole in country music that I could fill. I didn't dream there would be a million other people thinking the same thing. I was shocked by the sadness in singing music. There's 90 percent sadness and 10 percent happiness in this town. I'm thankful that I had the common sense to realize I wasn't supposed to be in Nashville at that time."

Garth went home, depressed and dejected. He stayed with his parents until he felt ready to start his career in earnest—and at the bottom of the heap. Moving back to Stillwater, he joined a country band called Santa Fe. Garth traveled with the group throughout the Southwest and learned about the business side of being a musician. He also proposed to Sandy. She said yes, and they were married in May 1986. Before long, the members of Santa Fe felt they were ready for a crack at the big time—they wanted to pack up and move to Nashville.

Garth knew by that time that he was committed to being a working musician. He was unafraid of the long hours, the sacrifices, and the hard work that is required of struggling artists. But he still hadn't quite forgotten the disappointment of his first trip to Nashville.

This time, though, Garth had someone at his side who believed in him, someone willing to work as hard and sacrifice as much as he did—Sandy. The young couple scraped together all of the money they had—$1,500—and moved to Nashville in 1987.

Before six months passed in Nashville, Santa Fe had broken up. Garth was depressed. He had no job, no band, and no recording contract. He and Sandy were living at the home of a friend, a songwriter named Bob Childress. Garth wanted to go back to Oklahoma, but Sandy said no. Garth recalls, "She just

Sandy supported Garth while he was trying to make it big in Nashville.

Nashville

sat me down and said, 'Look, I was around when you came back the last time, and I'm not going through that again. I think you're good enough and you think you're good enough, so we're going to stay right here. We'll get jobs, work, and live here, and you'll work on your music.'"

Through Sandy's strength, the couple persevered. One day they walked into a large Nashville store that sold fancy cowboy boots. The manager was from Texas, and he hired Garth and Sandy on the spot. Free from the worry of making ends meet, Garth worked hard, writing new songs and making contacts that would open doors for him in the capital of country music.

One of the Nashville insiders who believed in Garth was an ASCAP executive named Bob Doyle. He started a music-publishing firm, Major Bob Music, and paid Garth $300 per month to compose songs. Garth also found work as a singer on demo tapes for songwriters and as a jingle singer for radio and TV commercials. These jobs helped to give Garth confidence in himself as a working, professional musician. Early in 1988, Garth signed a contract making Bob Doyle and Pam Lewis, another smart, aggressive Nashville veteran, his managers.

Bob Doyle persuaded Lynn Shults, a talent scout for Capitol

Garth with Sandy and country legend Kitty Wells

Nashville

Records, to give Garth an audition. Shults's job was to discover singers and listen for new songs that might be good for artists on his record label. Shults liked what he heard, but he did not offer Garth a recording contract. Soon, however, he chanced to hear Garth perform live at the Bluebird Cafe, and that's when things began to change.

The Bluebird Cafe is a Nashville showcase for up-and-coming singers and songwriters. They perform new material in hopes of getting a song recorded by an established artist or of getting a recording contract themselves. Ever since his college days, Garth had been an exciting performer before a live audience. When he sang for Shults in his office at Capitol Records, he had been nervous. But this time he was completely relaxed. Garth mesmerized the Bluebird Cafe crowd with a dramatic rendition of his song "If Tomorrow Never Comes." Lynn Shults was so impressed he offered Garth a recording contract on the spot. Ten months after his arrival in Nashville, Garth Brooks was in the studio making his first album.

Four

The Phenomenon Begins

"Nothing ventured, nothing gained. Sometimes you've got to go against the grain."

—Garth Brooks, from "Against the Grain"

Garth Brooks's hero has always been John Wayne. "The Duke," as Wayne was called, was famous for his portrayals of heroic cowboys and military men and for his unwavering patriotism and devotion to all-American values. Garth idolized Wayne because he stood for what the singer described as total "honesty." And it was honesty that Garth wanted to communicate in his music. Garth was fortunate to find as his producer a man named Allen Reynolds. A Nashville veteran, he encouraged Garth to be true to himself. Reynolds wanted Garth to make each song come through as a pure expression of the singer's deepest feelings.

Working together, Garth and Allen Reynolds selected the songs for the singer's debut album, which was titled *Garth Brooks*. They felt strongly about the exquisite "If Tomorrow Never Comes," which Garth had co-written with Kent Blazy, a Nashville

Garth fools around, to the delight of his fans.

Garth Brooks Straight from the Heart

songwriter. The lyrics of "If Tomorrow Never Comes" advise people to declare their feelings for loved ones while they are still alive. While composing that song, Garth and Kent wondered if they had adequately told their wives how much they loved them. Garth also thought of his favorite track coach at Oklahoma State, who had died in an airplane crash. More recently, one of Garth's friends from college had been killed in an auto accident. "That song means a lot to me because of friends I've lost," Garth explains.

The album's opening song was "Not Counting You," a catchy number Garth had written by himself. Another selection was "Much Too Young (To Feel This Damn Old)." Although Garth grew up in the suburbs and is afraid of riding horseback, "Much Too Young" was the first of many songs he has recorded about rodeo riders. This song is about a man who has grown weary of life on the road, who yearns for a normal life with the woman he loves, whom he fears has left him.

Like Garth, Allen Reynolds liked dramatic songs that make strong statements about life and death, love and fear. Thus, Reynolds encouraged Garth to record a song written by Tony Arata called "The Dance." Although "The Dance" sounded less

Garth sings a heartfelt number.

like a traditional country tune than the other songs on the album, it became one of Garth's signature numbers, a song that people will always associate with Garth. Garth hates the meaningless kind of music he calls "ear candy." He prefers meaningful songs that touch people's deepest emotions and, perhaps, change their lives. "The Dance" is one of those songs. A heartfelt number, it is often played at funerals, not because it is sad, but because it celebrates life. "This song isn't about death," explains Garth. "It's about life, about doing everything you can with the time that God gives you."

Garth Brooks Straight from the Heart

Garth Brooks was released in 1989. Four of the album's songs became hits on the country music singles charts: "Not Counting You," "If Tomorrow Never Comes," "Much Too Young (To Feel This Damn Old)," and "The Dance." Garth Brooks was on his way. He was one of several promising young artists making his presence felt on a country music scene that was rapidly changing.

Ever since he was a little boy, Garth Brooks has been very competitive. He always wanted to throw the winning touchdown pass or strike out the last batter. And now, in 1990, he did not like being part of the herd, even if that "herd" was a small, elite group of gifted young musicians, who were breathing new life into country music.

Outside of Nashville, the national media called them "hat acts" because of their attire—cowboy boots, denim jeans, big-buckled belts, and ten-gallon Stetson hats like the ones the "singing cowboys" Gene Autry and Roy Rogers wore in the Western movies of the 1940s. But the term "hat act" also referred to their dedication to traditional country music.

It was older and purer strains of country music that inspired the so-called hat acts. This new breed of country singer was

The Phenomenon Begins

influenced by the Appalachian folk music of the Carter Family, the honky tonk of Hank Williams, Sr., and the bluesy song stylings of Johnny Cash, Patsy Cline, and George Jones.

Garth Brooks and his peers were *not* fond of the middle-of-the-road sounds that had been popular in Nashville since the late 1960s—tearful tunes that drowned the true soul of country in a sea of strings and favored lush orchestration over the sound of banjos, mandolins, and pedal steel guitars. Instead, Garth and musicians like him concentrated on writing simple, strong lyrics and composing straightforward, energetic music.

This attempt to renew country by returning to the music's roots was called the "new traditionalism." It had been started by artists like George Strait, Randy Travis, and Rodney Crowell, who were a few years older than Garth Brooks and his peers. Now the sounds of new traditionalism were being made by Garth and his contemporaries, performers like Alan Jackson, Suzy Bogguss, Travis Tritt, and Lorrie Morgan.

"As much as I hate the label a hat puts on you, if you take it off nobody knows who you are," Garth complained when he was struggling to carve out a niche for himself in country music. When Garth's singles were climbing the charts in late 1989,

Garth's music is so powerful because he really believes the words he sings.

music industry experts felt that country's next big superstar was going to be Clint Black, a handsome and gifted singer-songwriter who had been born in Houston, Texas, just three days after Garth. Moreover, Black's first album, *Killin' Time*, was released at almost exactly the same time in 1989 as *Garth Brooks*.

Garth admits he was jealous of the praise that was showered on Black. He did not want to be thought of as "Garth Black," as a newspaper in Texas once mistakenly called him!

It was Garth's showmanship that allowed him to burst out of the crowd. No country performer ever displayed such flair and

The Phenomenon Begins

dynamism on stage. While working on his debut album, Garth also assembled a band. He wanted to play with musicians who would have the right chemistry, which Garth calls "the most essential element in a good band." He recruited the guitar players James Garver, Steve McClure, and Ty Englund, drummer Mike Palmer, and keyboardist and fiddler Dave Gant. When his sister, Betsy, came aboard as bass guitarist, the group was complete. In honor of his old college town, Garth named his band Stillwater.

From the very beginning, Garth loved performing with Stillwater. On stage, he says, is "where my heart beats fastest" and "my blood rushes." "First, you were the underdog, and it didn't much matter what you'd do; people were nice to you," Garth says about his early days on the road with Stillwater. "But now we're on a level where we have to go into a lot of places and turn around a crowd that maybe doesn't like you because you wear a hat. Or thinks, 'Well, this guy's just a shadow of Clint Black.'

"So, you go out there and start working and see 'em start to shift, and by the end of the show you're looking around, and your guitar player's screaming at you from ten feet away and you can only see his mouth moving; you can't hear nothin' except this

Garth Brooks Straight from the Heart

crowd. That's when your heart gets to pumping so hard you take your guitar and throw it as hard as you can across the stage, and the crowd goes nuts.

"Then you do something else to make 'em go nuts, and it starts passing back and forth, and you get more fired up than the crowd does. Then it gets into just total mania. . . . Then the show's over, and you're sitting back on the bus going, 'Holy Cow! What just happened?'

"It's great. I wouldn't trade it for the world."

Garth also outdistanced the rest of the hat pack through his remarkable ability to record songs that, almost overnight, became country music standards. "If Tomorrow Never Comes" was that kind of song, so was "The Dance." And in 1990, while working on his second album, Garth recorded another instant classic, "Friends in Low Places." Written by Dewayne Blackwell and Earl Bud Lee, "Friends in Low Places" is about a jilted "redneck" who shows up uninvited at his ex-girlfriend's formal wedding dinner. As recorded by Garth, "Friends in Low Places" is a rowdy saloon sing-along that takes a humorous look at the foibles of unrequited love.

With "Friends in Low Places" already soaring on the country

Garth jams with his band.

singles charts, Garth's *No Fences* was released in August 1990. The album contained three number one hit songs in addition to "Friends": "The Thunder Rolls," "Two of a Kind Workin' on a Full House," and "Unanswered Prayers." Ten days after its release, more than 700,000 copies of *No Fences* had been sold. Several weeks later Capitol Records announced that the first album, *Garth Brooks,* had achieved platinum status, meaning that more than one million copies had been sold.

Garth Brooks was no longer in the shadows of anyone in country music. Now he was the one casting the shadow.

Five

Ropin' the Wind

*"This ain't comin' from no prophet,
just an ordinary man."*

—Garth Brooks, from "We Shall Be Free"

In October 1990 a lifelong dream of Garth's came true when the Grand Ole Opry made him its 65th member. Only the legendary Hank Williams, Sr., had been inducted into the Grand Ole Opry at an earlier age than the 28-year-old from Yukon. Garth's hometown celebrated his success by putting his name on a water tower, and the Country Music Hall of Fame asked him to donate one of the ten-gallon hats and striped shirts that he loves to wear when he straps on his acoustic guitar and starts to sing.

The Country Music Association Awards show is one of Nashville's most important annual events. Held at the Grand Ole Opry and broadcast to a national television audience, the CMA Awards are Nashville's equivalent of the Oscar ceremonies in Hollywood. In the autumn of 1990 Garth was nominated for five coveted awards: Male Vocalist of the Year, the Horizon Award for

*Garth collects presents from
his fans during a show.*

Garth Brooks Straight from the Heart

best new artist, Single of the Year as well as Song of the Year for "If Tomorrow Never Comes," and Best Video of the Year for "The Dance."

Garth and Sandy watched from the audience as other artists marched triumphantly to the stage. Clint Black won the award for the year's best male vocalist. Vince Gill's "When I Call Your Name" beat out "If Tomorrow Never Comes" for Best Single. Kathy Mattea's "Where've You Been?" was named Song of the Year. But Garth was pleased when his song won for Best Video—and overjoyed when he received the Horizon Award. Taking Sandy's hand, he led her to stage with him. "I'm not much good at it," said Garth as he accepted the best new artist award, "but when I don't sing, I try and be a husband. This is my wife, Sandy. I want to thank the good Lord because He's done a hell of a lot for me."

Garth did not mean that he feels blessed in ways other singers are not. He is thankful for his musical talent and awed that he is able to make a living doing what he loves. A patriotic man with a strong religious faith, Garth once told his parents that his ambition as a singer was to return prayer to dinner tables all across America. Although that goal remains unaccomplished,

A tearful Garth thanks Sandy for her support while accepting the Country Music Association's Horizon Award.

Garth himself was unprepared for the milestone he was to reach in 1991.

By Christmas 1990 *No Fences* had climbed to the number one spot on the country music charts. It also held the number twelve position on *Billboard*'s listing of pop albums, making Garth's the most popular country album in five years, since *Trio* by Dolly Parton, Linda Ronstadt, and Emmylou Harris had been a crossover pop-country hit. Nashville insiders now recognized

Garth and Sandy at a celebration for the success of Ropin' the Wind.

that Garth's success was no fluke. He appealed to people who rarely listened to country, as well as country's die-hard fans. *No Fences* had gone triple platinum when the time came for the Academy of Country Music Awards in April 1991.

The night of the show, Garth won an unprecedented six "hats," as the Academy of Country Music calls its awards. He was named Entertainer of the Year and Male Vocalist of the Year. "Friends in Low Places" won for Best Single and *No Fences* for

Ropin' the Wind

Best Album. He received two more "hats" for "The Dance," which was named Song of the Year and Video of the Year.

In the summer of 1990, Garth had at one point given concerts on 52 consecutive days. Garth works harder on stage than most performers because he wants even the fans who sit in the last row to "feel special." He even reserves the first two rows at every show for a special group of fans. Before each show, Garth's staff finds the people with the worst seats and moves them up front, where they can enjoy their hero up close.

Garth's hectic performance schedule continued in 1991, when he made some 200 live appearances with Stillwater. Somehow Garth also found the time to work in the studio, where he recorded the most popular country album of all time—*Ropin' the Wind*.

Country music has been called the "white man's blues." It developed out of English folk ballads, gospel music, and the "cowboy songs" of the western plains. Country music has always been popular in the South and rural portions of the Midwest, but the sounds of Nashville had limited national appeal after the death of Hank Williams, Sr., in the early 1950s. A few years later Elvis Presley, a southerner who had grown up singing country

Garth Brooks Straight from the Heart

and gospel songs, put rock 'n' roll on the charts, where it has stayed ever since.

In the 1980s the most popular American singers were Michael Jackson, a black soul singer, and Bruce Springsteen, a white rock 'n' roller. No country recording had ever been number one on the *Billboard* pop album charts—until Garth Brooks made *Ropin' the Wind*.

With more than two million advance orders from record stores, Garth's third album *entered* the pop charts at Number One the day it was released: September 23, 1991. Garth called *Ropin' the Wind* a "postcards-from-the-edge album—every song is pretty much out there on a limb." Although some music critics felt that the album lacked any numbers as good as "Friends in Low Places" or "If Tomorrow Never Comes," Garth's fans were delighted by new songs like "What She's Doing Now," "We Bury the Hatchet," "Papa Loved Mama," and "Rodeo."

Like a baseball pitcher, Garth throws an occasional curveball at his fans. For example, on *No Fences* he had included "Mr. Blue," a song the vocal group the Fleetwoods had popularized in the 1950s. On *Ropin' the Wind*, Garth covered "Shameless," an ode to unrequited love that had been written by Billy Joel.

Fans swarm around Garth's tour bus.

"Shameless," Garth explains, is about someone who is willing to say: "I'd crawl ten yards through broken glass on my hands and knees just for you to kick me in the face."

At the Country Music Association Awards ceremonies in October 1991, Garth was expected to be the big winner. So it was no surprise when *No Fences* was named Album of the Year and "Friends in Low Places" won for Single of the Year. Moreover, Garth was named Entertainer of the Year, which is country music's most prestigious award. Garth became the first performer to win the Horizon Award for best newcomer one year and then be named Entertainer of the Year the next.

Garth Brooks Straight from the Heart

But what Garth wanted most was for "The Thunder Rolls" to be named Best Video of the Year.

Garth has declared that he refuses to make a music video that is a "no-brainer," and his videos are unlike those of any other country performer. In his video of "The Dance," he included film footage of his three American heroes: John Wayne, President John F. Kennedy, and the Reverend Martin Luther King, Jr. However, Nashville is a conservative town. And for his "The Thunder Rolls" video Garth took creative risks that fueled the biggest controversy of his career.

"The Thunder Rolls" is about a womanizer, a married man who cannot keep his hands off other women. Garth himself played the part of the cheating husband, a vile man who also abuses his wife. The climax of the video shows Garth's character coming home drunk. He beats his wife and is about to turn his rage on his daughter when his wife guns him down with a .38-caliber pistol. Angered by the violence, Sandy had wanted Garth to change the video, which contained visual images not implied in the song's lyrics. He refused, and the video was released in its original version in the spring of 1991.

"The Thunder Rolls" became the first video to be banned by

the two cable television networks that broadcast country music videos: Country Music Television (CMT) and The Nashville Network (TNN). Garth's response was diplomatic. "I would have never, ever done something TNN and CMT couldn't use," he explained, "but I'm not going to change what I do to fit their standards." However, he later admitted that the banning of his video had "crushed" him. "I was shocked," Garth said. "I was so hurt."

Garth was vindicated by the members of the Country Music Association, who voted "The Thunder Rolls" the Best Video of the Year. He had stuck to his guns, just as John Wayne would have wanted Garth to, and refused to compromise. After all, it was Garth's sincerity, the kind that cannot be faked, that his fans sensed and responded to when he sang. Garth said of those who banned his video, "They want to see the good side of real life, but they want to turn their backs to the bad side." "The Thunder Rolls" video is widely used by counselors at shelters for battered women throughout the United States to help women who have been victimized deal with their anger. For Garth, this is the greatest award of all.

Conclusion

Welcome to the Nineties

"As long as it brings an emotion, then you know you're living."

—Garth Brooks on music that speaks to the heart

Looking directly into the camera, the singer said, "We're going to try to show you what a Garth Brooks is. I know what you're thinking: Dull." The image on the television screen changed to concert footage of Garth playing the drums with the neck of his guitar. "Boring," he said. Now the picture showed him dancing downstage. "Old hat." Garth was pouring water over his head. "Like watching paint dry." Garth and one of Stillwater's guitar players smashed their acoustics together in midair. "Welcome to the nineties."

That was Garth's way of introducing himself to a national television audience when NBC broadcast "This Is Garth Brooks" on January 9, 1992. Consisting of footage from a concert in Dallas the previous fall, Garth's hour-long show drew more Friday night viewers to NBC than at any time since the middle

Garth belts out a song.

Garth Brooks Straight from the Heart

1980s, when "Miami Vice" was a hit TV series. On the concert circuit, Garth was setting attendance records in the South and Southwest. More than 23,000 tickets were snapped in just 77 minutes for a Garth show in Charlotte, North Carolina. He sold out the 10,000-seat Murphy Center in Murfreesboro, Tennessee, in a record 21 minutes. For a show at the Reunion Arena in Dallas, Texas, 18,000 tickets were purchased in 37 minutes, breaking a record held by Bruce Springsteen.

It's hard to believe. A balding guy with a cowboy hat, an acoustic guitar, and a southern accent is as big a singing star as Madonna, Prince, Whitney Houston, or Michael Jackson.

Why did Garth Brooks suddenly become the most popular entertainer in the history of country music? A writer for the *New York Times* said that Garth's success derives from his "meat-and-potatoes image" and his "virtuous, all-American values."

Other writers have noted that Garth's music appeals to members of the Baby Boom generation who were raised on rock 'n' roll. Those "fortysomethings" hear the influence on Garth of folk-pop musicians they loved two decades earlier, singers like James Taylor, Paul Simon, and Joni Mitchell. They also respond to the rowdy, driving energy of songs like "Friends in

Garth's loyal fans have made him music's number one star.

Low Places." And many people of all age groups care little for the sounds that nowadays dominate the MTV airwaves: dance music with its repetitive, computerized beat and insipid lyrics, rap songs that are aggressively confrontational, and heavy metal, which is loud and monotonous. Garth's songs, on the other hand, have clever lyrics and shiny melodies. More important, each of Garth's songs has a message that he conveys with emotions that are strong and pure.

Garth himself gives the best explanation of his music's extraordinary appeal. "The one thing everybody in this world

Former president George Bush congratulates Garth and other performers at the 1991 Country Music Association Awards.

has in common is that they have a heart," he says. "They might not speak the same language or listen to the same music, but they've got hearts. You're drivin' down the road and the music comes on, and it moves you and makes you think. As long as it brings an emotion, then you know you're living."

In November 1991 Garth announced that Sandy was pregnant and that he was taking a six-month break from touring with Stillwater. Spending time with Sandy at their home outside

58

Conclusion: Welcome to the Nineties

Nashville, Garth also worked on new songs and spent time in the recording studio putting together two new albums that he planned to release later in 1992. In February Garth won a Grammy Award for Best Male Vocal Performance, and in March he appeared with Stillwater as a musical guest on NBC's popular "Saturday Night Live."

On weekends, Garth prepared his band for a 77-city concert tour that began on June 2 at the McNichols Arena in Denver, Colorado, and was scheduled to end on December 12 at the Palace in Auburn Hills, Michigan. Released in September, Garth's fourth album, *The Chase*, shot straight to the top of the charts. Garth pleased both country and pop fans with songs like "We Shall Be Free," a plea for tolerance and racial harmony that he co-wrote with Stephanie Davis, and with cover versions of the bluesy "Walkin' After Midnight," which Patsy Cline had recorded more than three decades earlier, and the rollicking "Dixie Chicken," which the rock group Little Feat had popularized in the 1970s. Later in the year, Garth released *Beyond the Season*, a Yuletide offering that included seasonal standards such as "White Christmas" and "Silent Night."

In the summer of 1992, Sandy had given birth to Taylor

Garth Brooks Straight from the Heart

Mayne Brooks. She was named after James Taylor, Garth's musical idol, and for the state of Maine, where Sandy and her husband believed their first child had been conceived. Garth, however, began to resent the way his career kept him away from his wife and baby girl. In an interview with Jane Pauley of the NBC news magazine "Dateline," Garth shocked his fans. Frustrated by the relentless demands of fame and show business, he said that he might retire to become a full-time husband and father.

A few days later Garth performed "We Shall Be Free" on "Tonight." Talking to the show's host, Jay Leno, Garth explained why he had mixed feelings about being a superstar. "When I looked at my baby girl, I knew God put me down here to be a parent," he said. "But then I do a song with the band, and I know He put me down here to play music, too." Garth said if he could not give "110 percent" of himself to his music *and* to being a father, he would have to make a choice. "And," he declared, "you can't choose against your own flesh and blood."

It seems likely that Garth will, somehow, find a way to reconcile the demands of parenthood with the demands of his career. Of course, being Garth Brooks, music superstar and

Conclusion: Welcome to the Nineties

country folk hero, is not an ordinary job. His millions of fans want him to buoy their hopes and sustain their dreams, to use a magnificent palette in bringing color to the gray areas of their lives.

But Garth Brooks is an artist of limitless ambition. His love of playing and singing is simple and joyous. He truly believes that his talent and success are gifts. "The most priceless thing I could lose would be the chance to sing," Garth once said. "It's a wonderful way to make a living." It is hard to believe that Garth will simply walk away when there is so much more that he has left to do. That's the kind of man Garth Brooks is. The kind who gives nothing less than 110 percent to the things he loves.

Discography

Garth Brooks 1989 (Liberty Records)

No Fences 1990 (Liberty Records)

Ropin' the Wind 1991 (Liberty Records)

Beyond the Season 1992 (Liberty Records)

The Chase 1992 (Liberty Records)

Index

Academy of Country Music Awards, 48
ASCAP, 27, 31

Beyond the Season, 59
Black, Clint, 40, 41, 46
Blazy, Kent, 35, 36
Bogguss, Suzy, 39
Brooks Colleen), 11, 12, 18, 19, 25
Brooks, Garth: as an athlete, 14, 15, 18, 21, 22, 23; birth of, 11; as a college student, 19, 21, 22, 23, 25; as a high-school student, 14, 15, 17, 18; showmanship of, 18, 40, 42, 49; song lyrics of, 14, 36, 37, 39, 42, 51, 52, 57
Brooks, Kelly, 11
Brooks, Mike, 11
Brooks, Sandy Mahr, 22, 23, 25, 29, 31, 46, 52, 58, 59, 60
Brooks, Taylor Maine, 59-60
Brooks, Troyal Raymond (Ray), 11, 12, 14, 18, 25

Capitol Records, 7, 12, 31, 33, 43
Cline, Patsy, 39, 59
Country Music Association Awards, 45, 51, 53
Country Music Hall of Fame, 45
Country Music Television (CMT), 53
Crowell, Rodney, 39

"Dance, The," 36, 37, 38, 42, 46, 49, 52

Englund, Ty, 41
Entertainer of the Year award, 51

Fogelberg, Dan, 17
"Friends in Low Places," 42, 43, 48, 50, 51, 56

Garth Brooks, 35, 38, 40, 43
Grammy Award for Best Male Vocal Performance, 59
Grand Ole Opry, 45

Littlefield, Merlin, 27, 28
Los Angeles, California, 8
Madonna, 7, 8, 56
Major Bob Music, 31

Mattea, Kathy, 46
McClure, Steve, 41
Mitchell, Joni, 56
"Mr. Blue," 50
"Much Too Young (To Feel This Damn Old)," 36, 38

Nashville Network, The (TNN), 53
Nashville, Tennessee, 7, 25, 27, 28, 29, 31, 33, 38, 39, 45, 49, 52, 59
No Fences, 43, 47, 48, 50, 51
"Not Counting You," 36, 38

Oklahoma State University, 19, 21, 22, 36
Opryland USA, 25

"Papa Loved Mama," 50
Presley, Elvis, 8-9, 49
Prince, 56

Reynolds, Allen, 25, 36
Ropin' the Wind, 7, 49, 50

Santa Fe, 29
"Saturday Night Live," 59
"Shameless," 50, 51
Simon, Paul, 56
Smittle, Betsy, 11, 14, 41
Smittle, Jerry, 11
Smittle, Jim, 11
Springsteen, Bruce, 50, 56
Stillwater, 41, 49, 55, 58, 59
Strait, George, 18, 39

Taylor, James, 17, 56, 60
"This Is Garth Brooks," 55
"Two of a Kind Workin' on a Full House," 43

"Walkin' After Midnight," 59
"We Bury the Hatchet," 50
"We Shall Be Free," 59, 60
"What She's Doing Now, 50

Yukon High School, 14, 19
Yukon, Oklahoma, 12, 25, 45

About the Author

Edward Tallman is a freelance writer and biographer of filmmakers, musicians, and current sports folk heroes. He has worked as an editor at St. Martin's Press and the H. W. Wilson Company, where he published several award-winning reference books on the subjects of modern art and the American presidency.

Ed is currently breathing the fresh air of Garth Brooks country in the Appalachian Mountains of West Virginia.